BE Strong & Courageous do not be afraid, for the Lord goes with you wherever you go!

Joshua 1:9

I am a new Creation

2 Corinthians 5:17

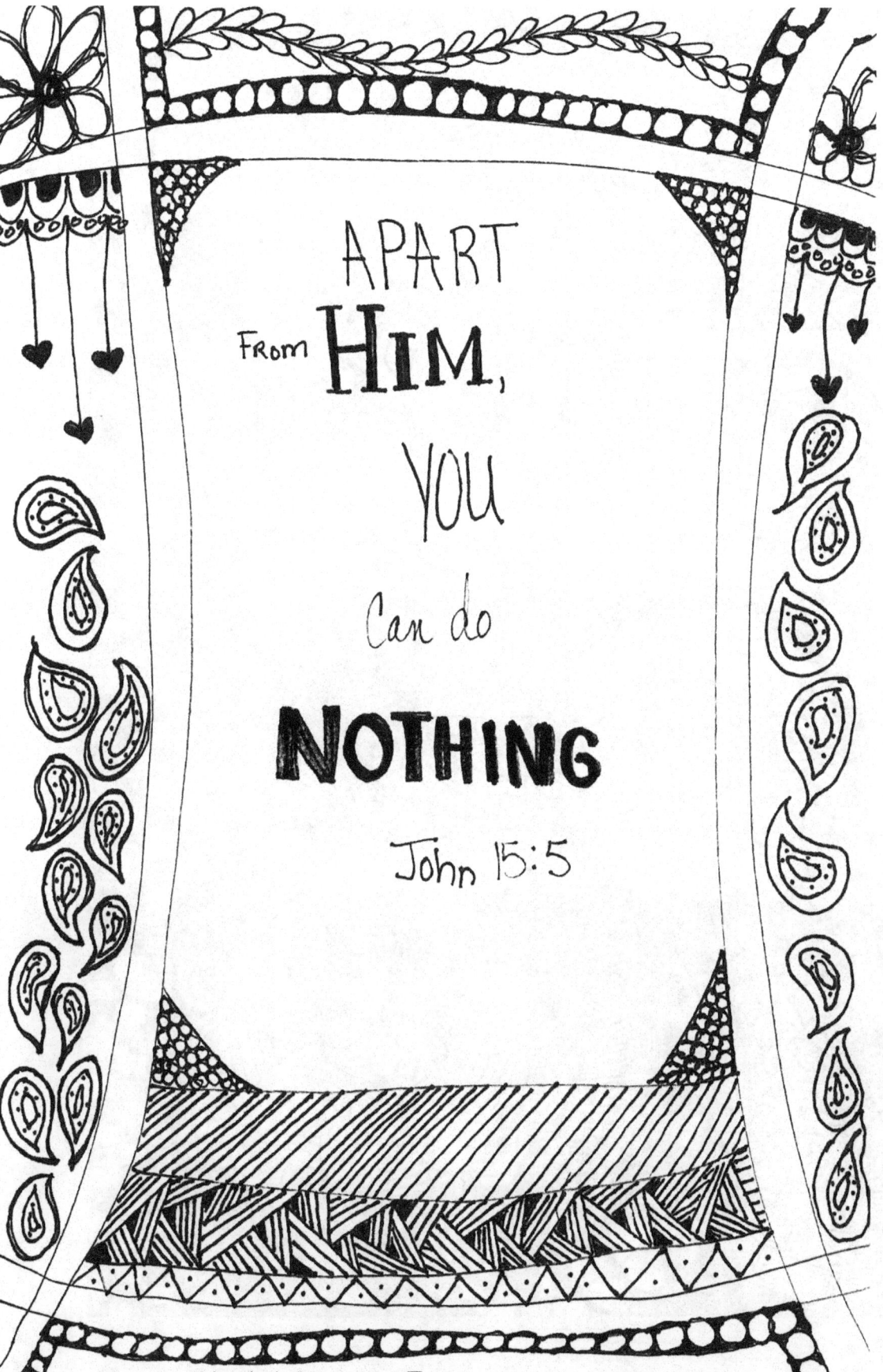

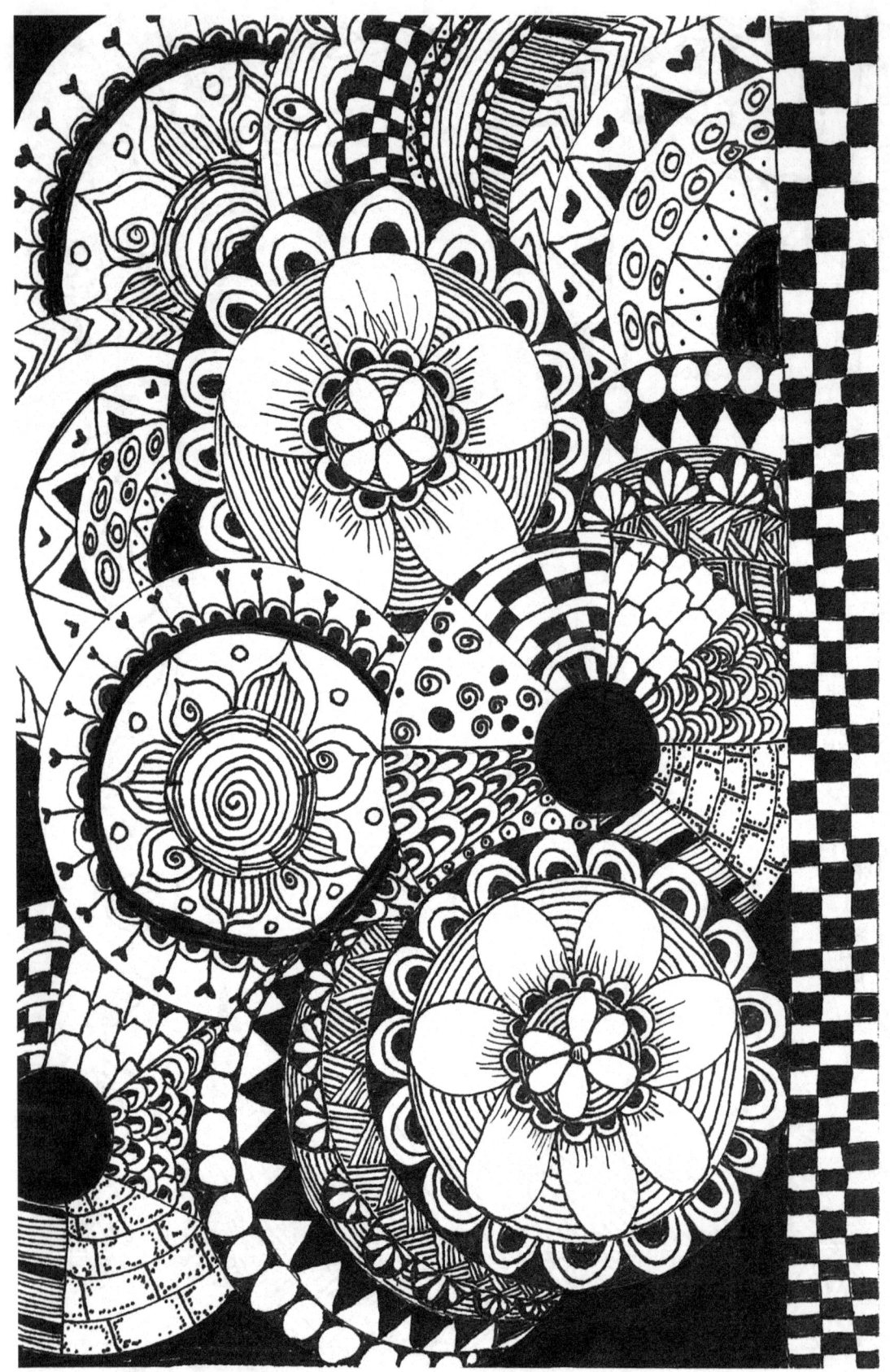

Don't forget whose you are! #KingsKid

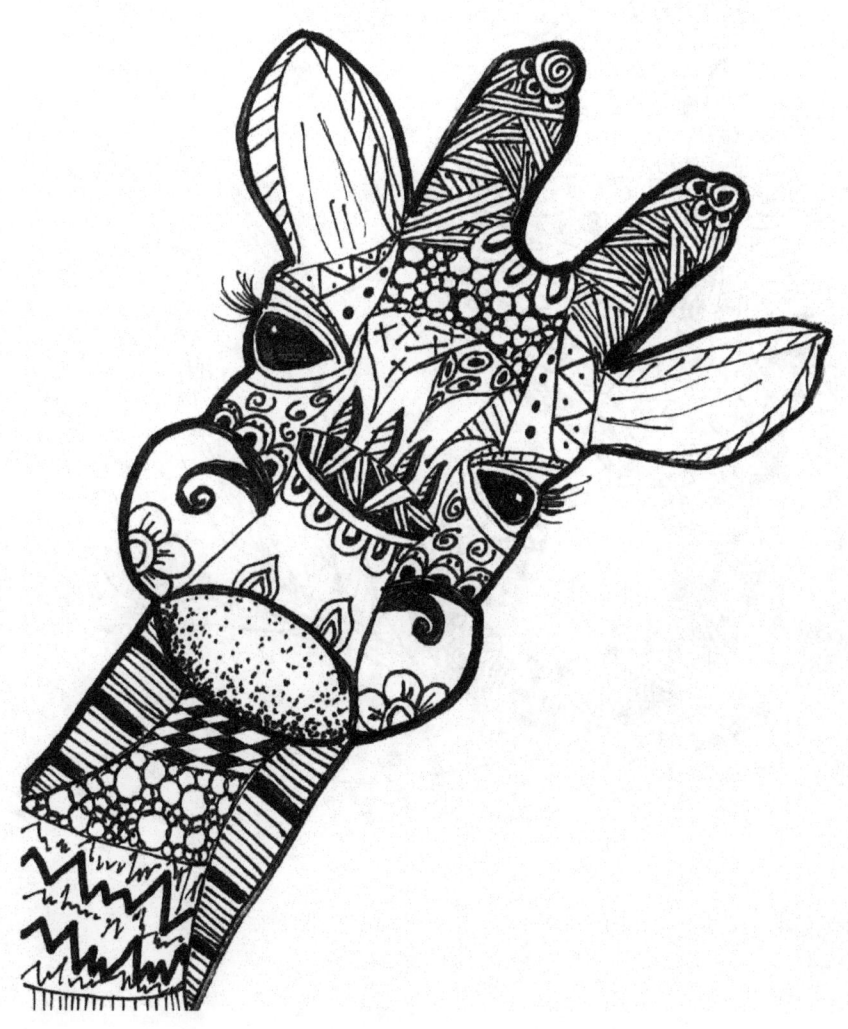

Praise the LORD from the earth, You great **sea** creatures.

Psalm 148:7

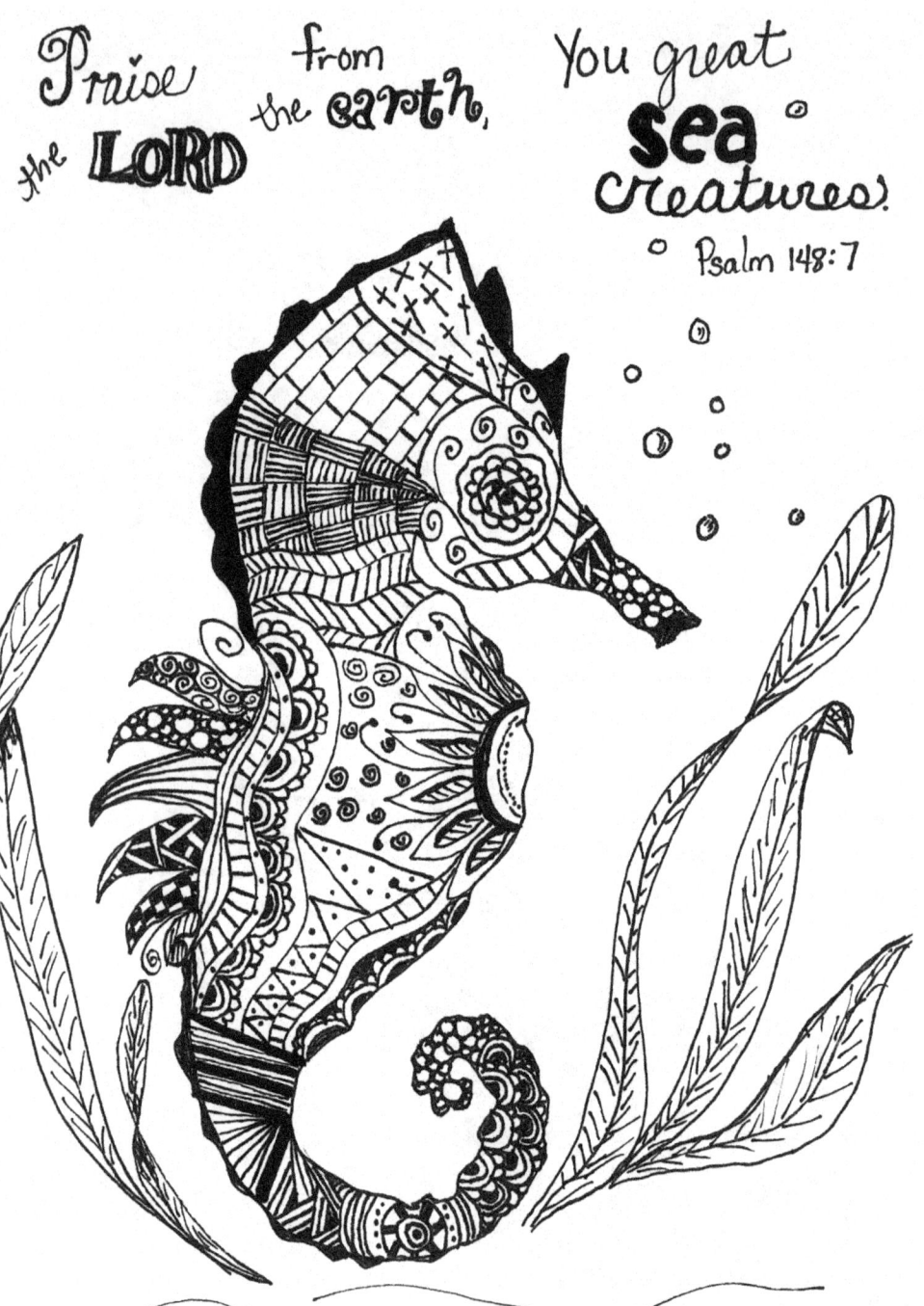

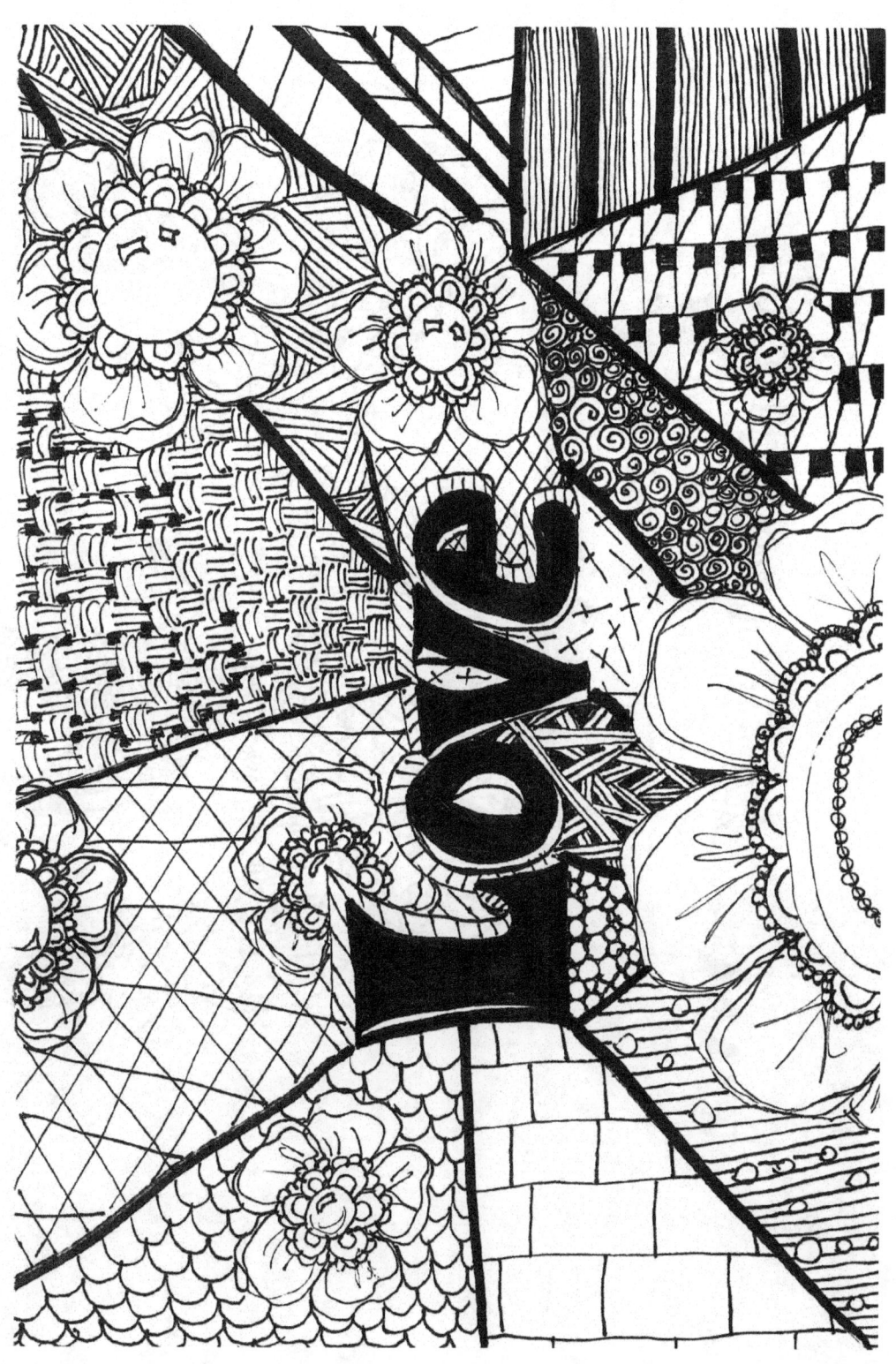

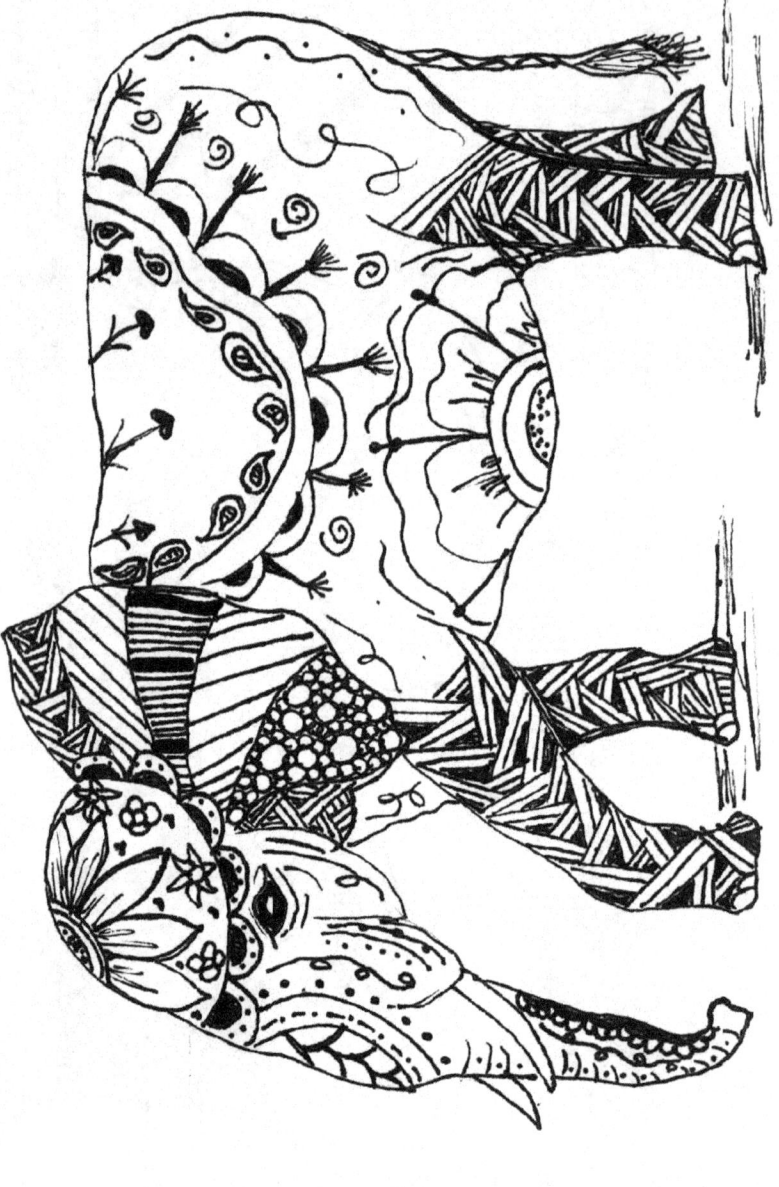

I AM fearfully & wonderfully Made ♡
Psalm 139:14b ☺

The LORD has done Great things FOR US! Psalm 126:3

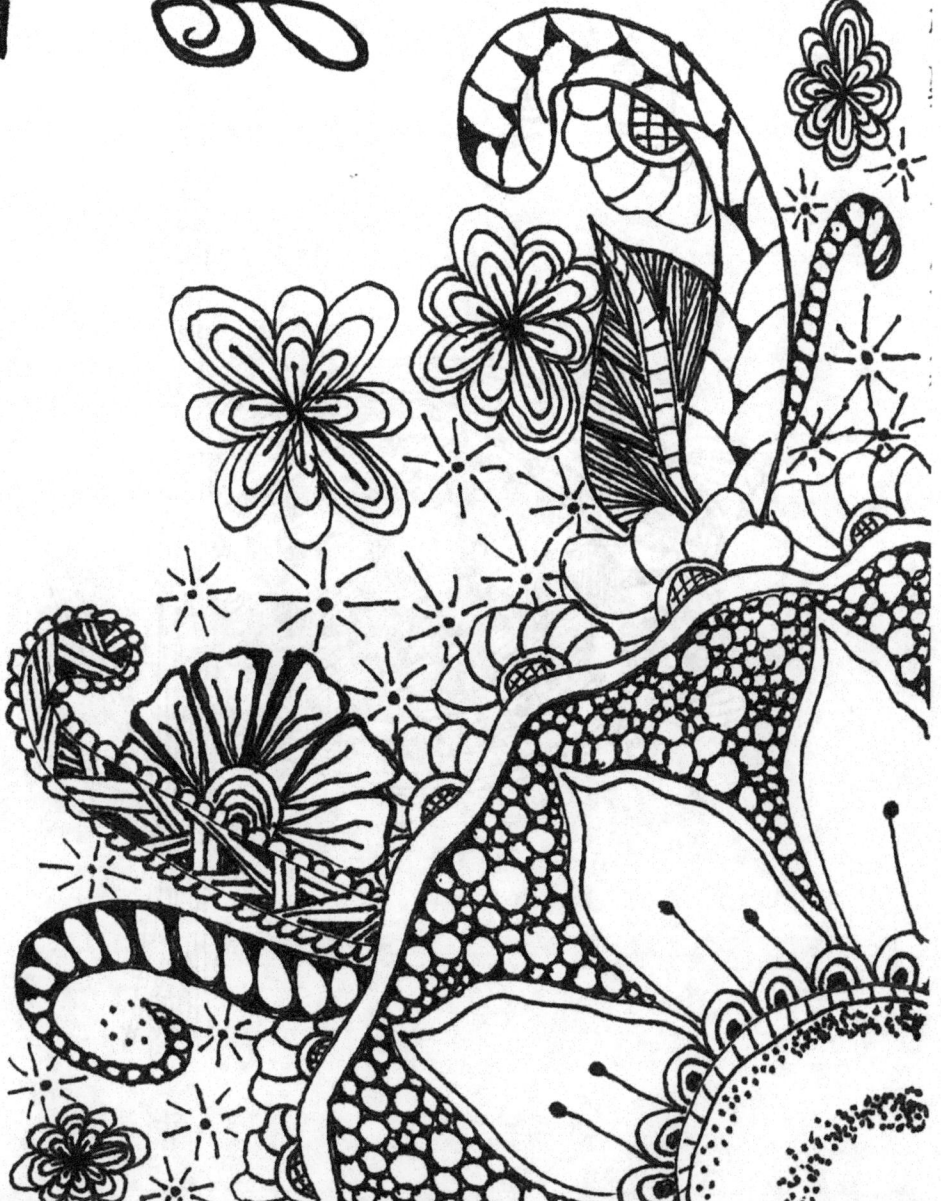

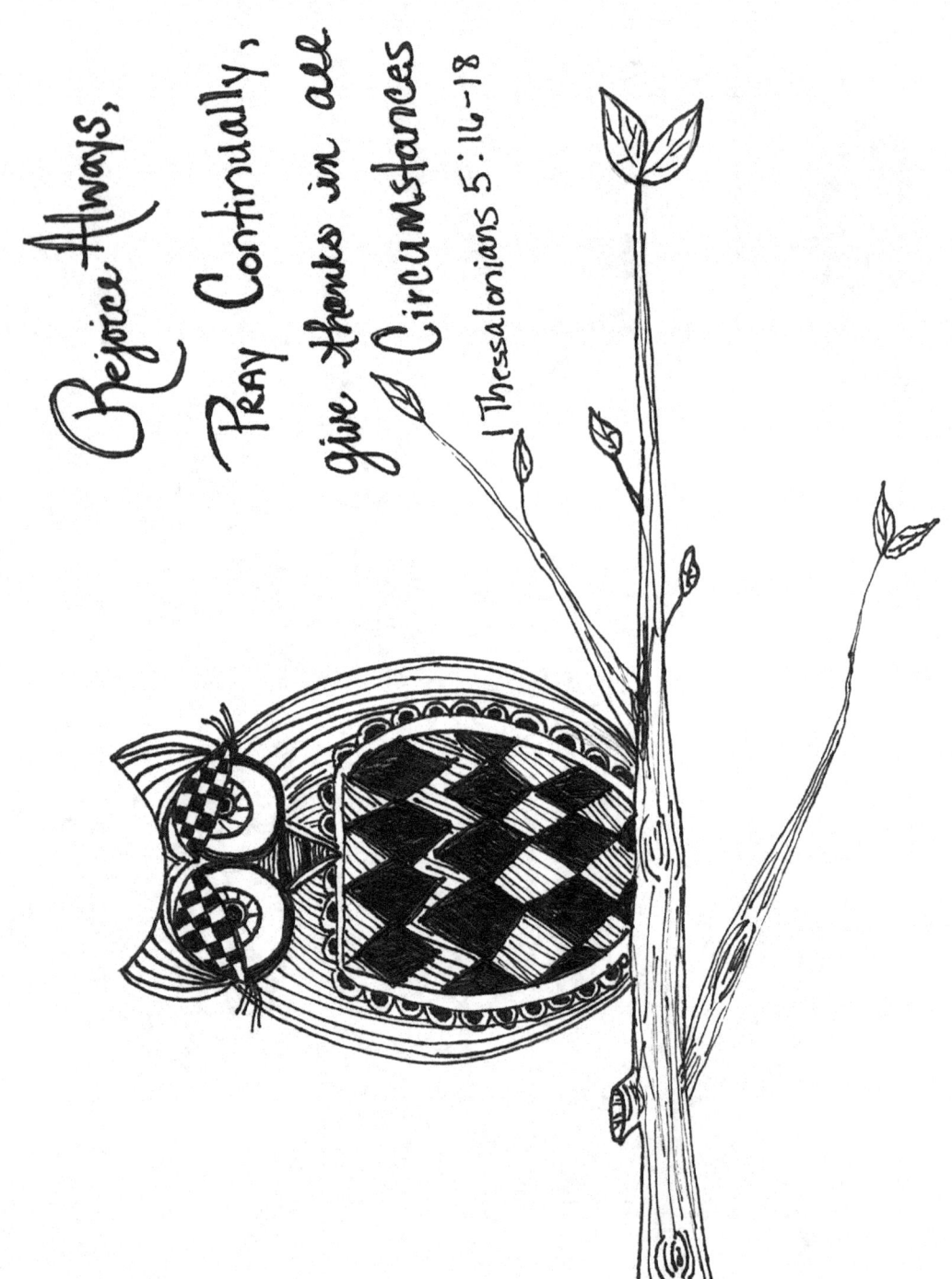

Rejoice Always,
Pray Continually,
give thanks in all
Circumstances
1 Thessalonians 5:16-18

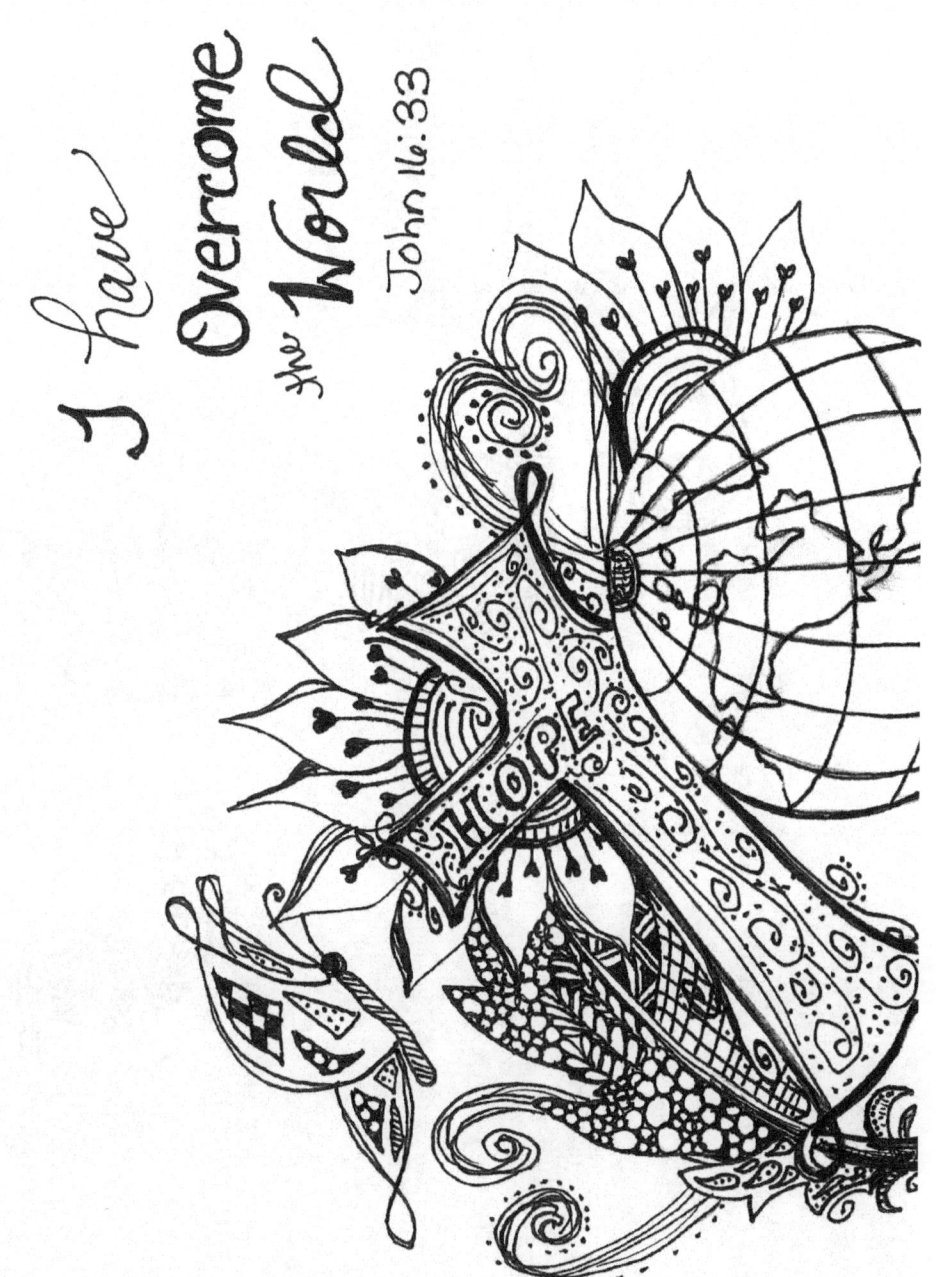

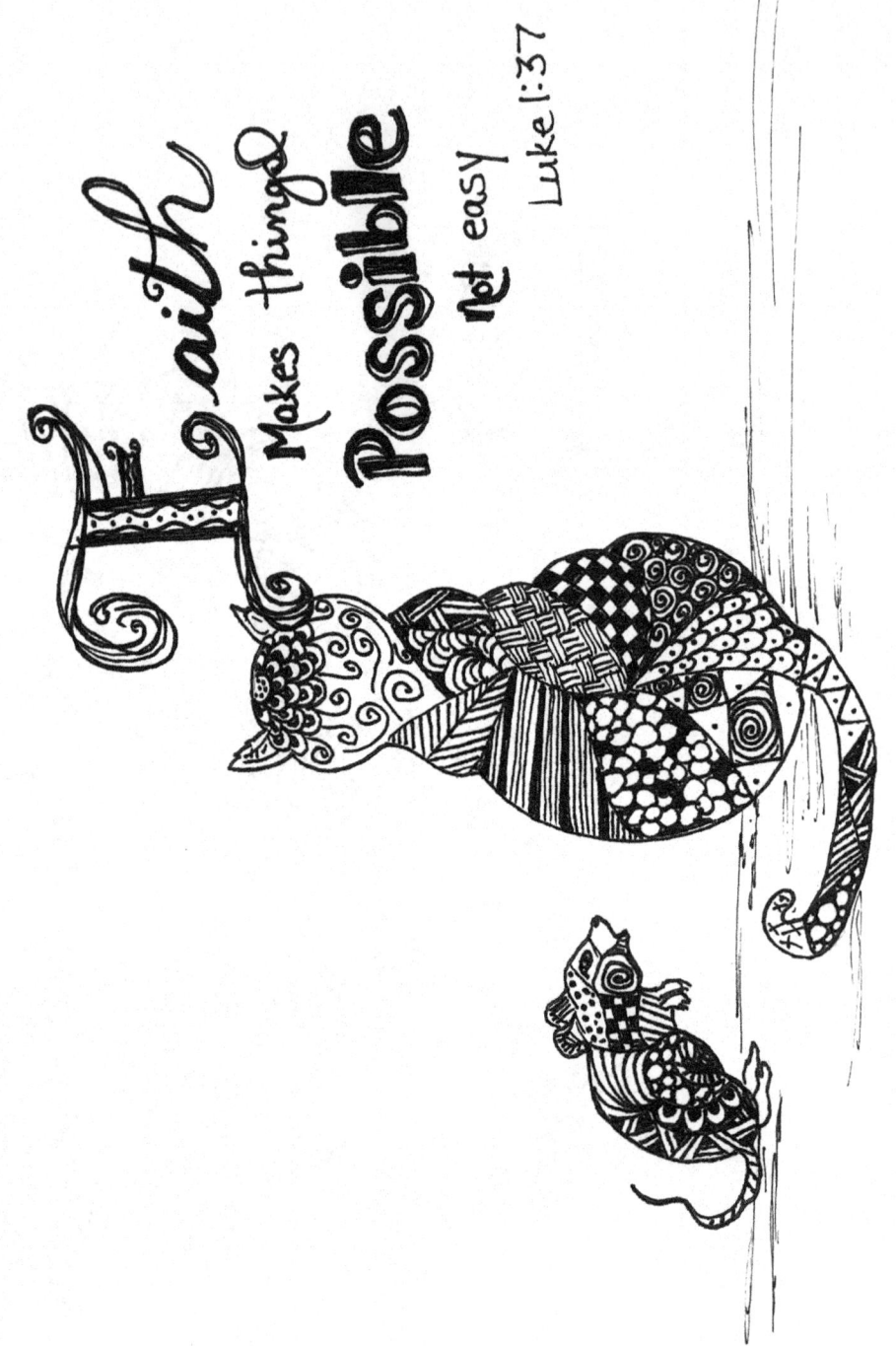

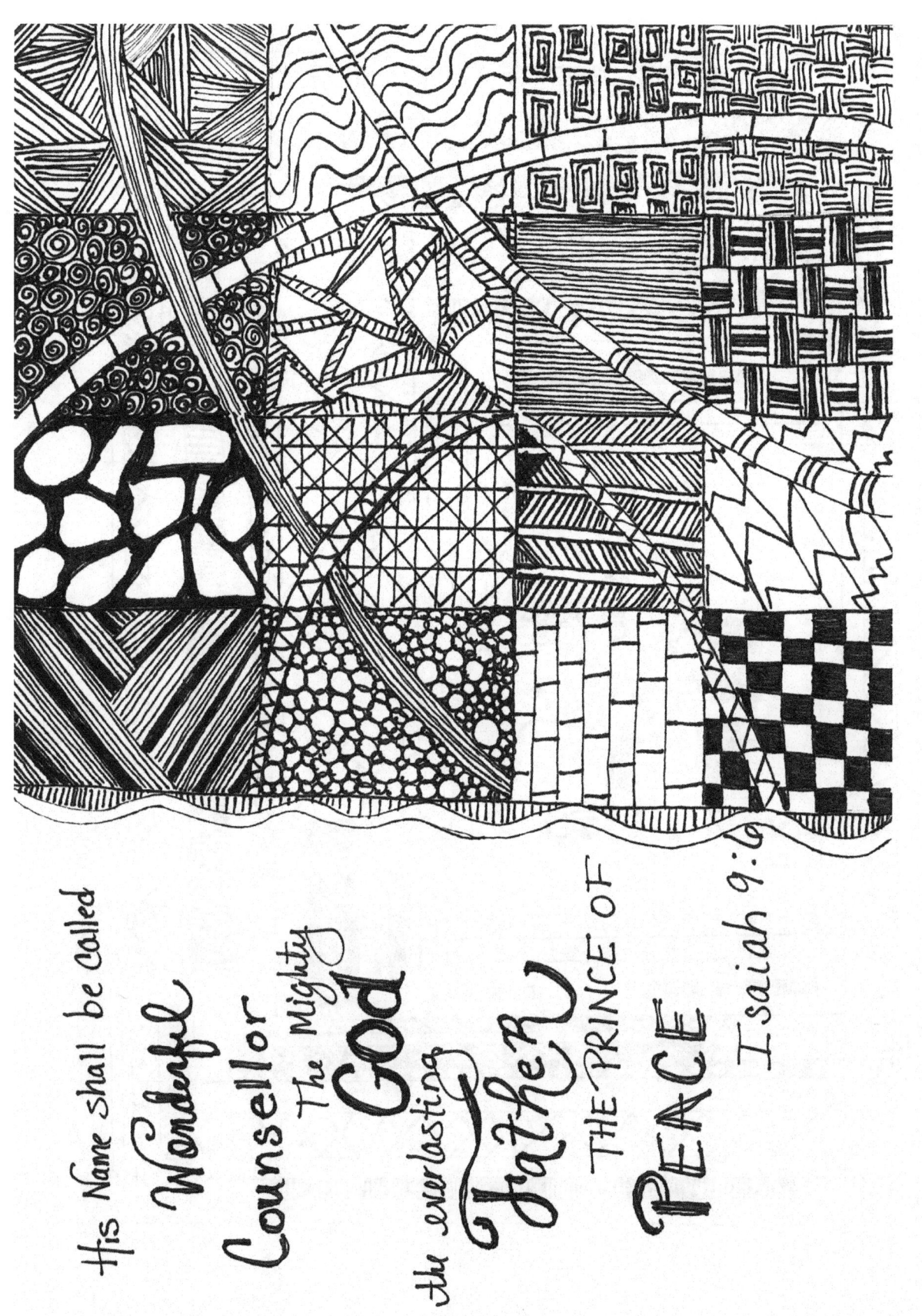

His Name shall be called
Wonderful
Counsellor
The Mighty
God
the everlasting
Father
THE PRINCE OF
PEACE
Isaiah 9:6

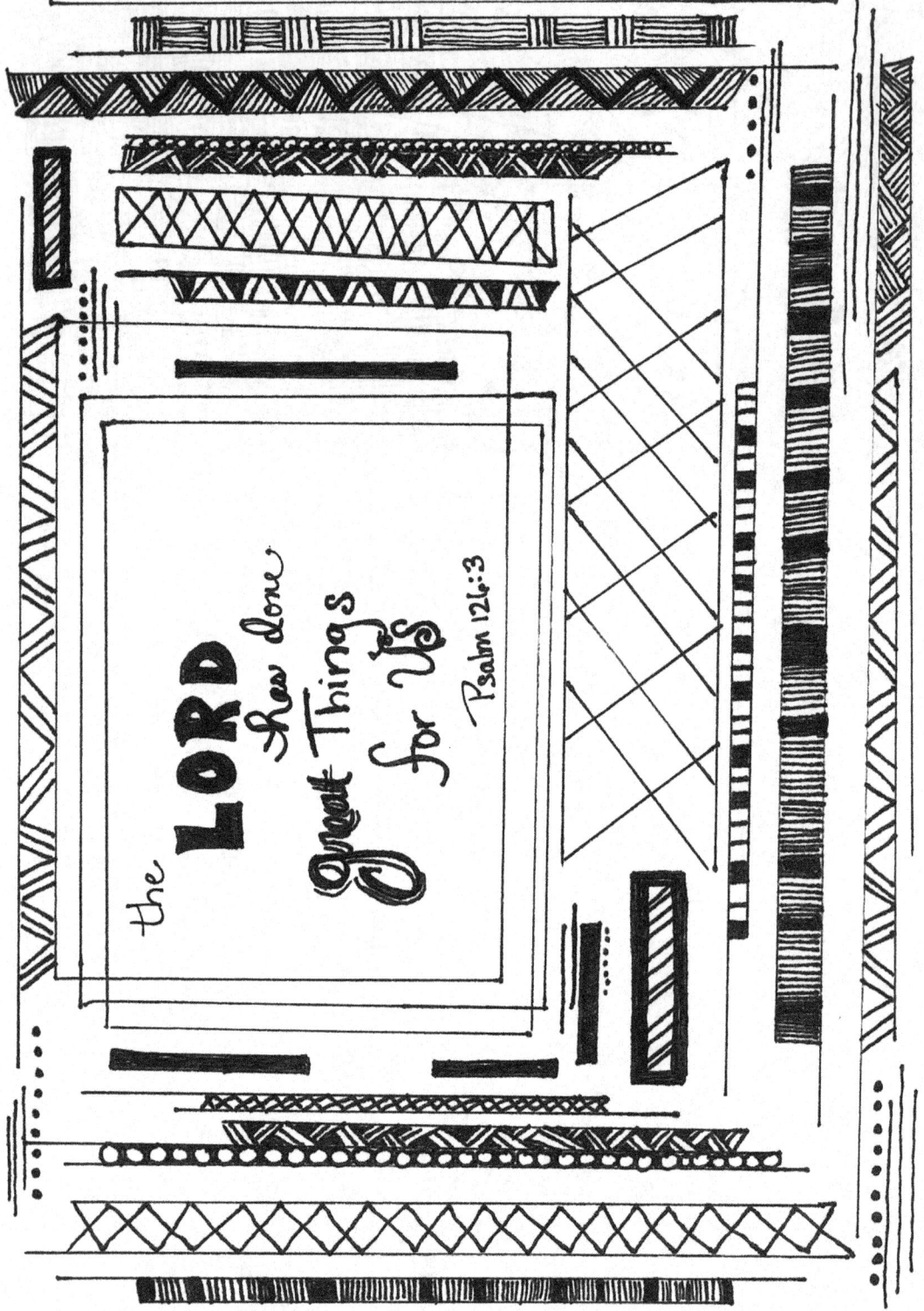

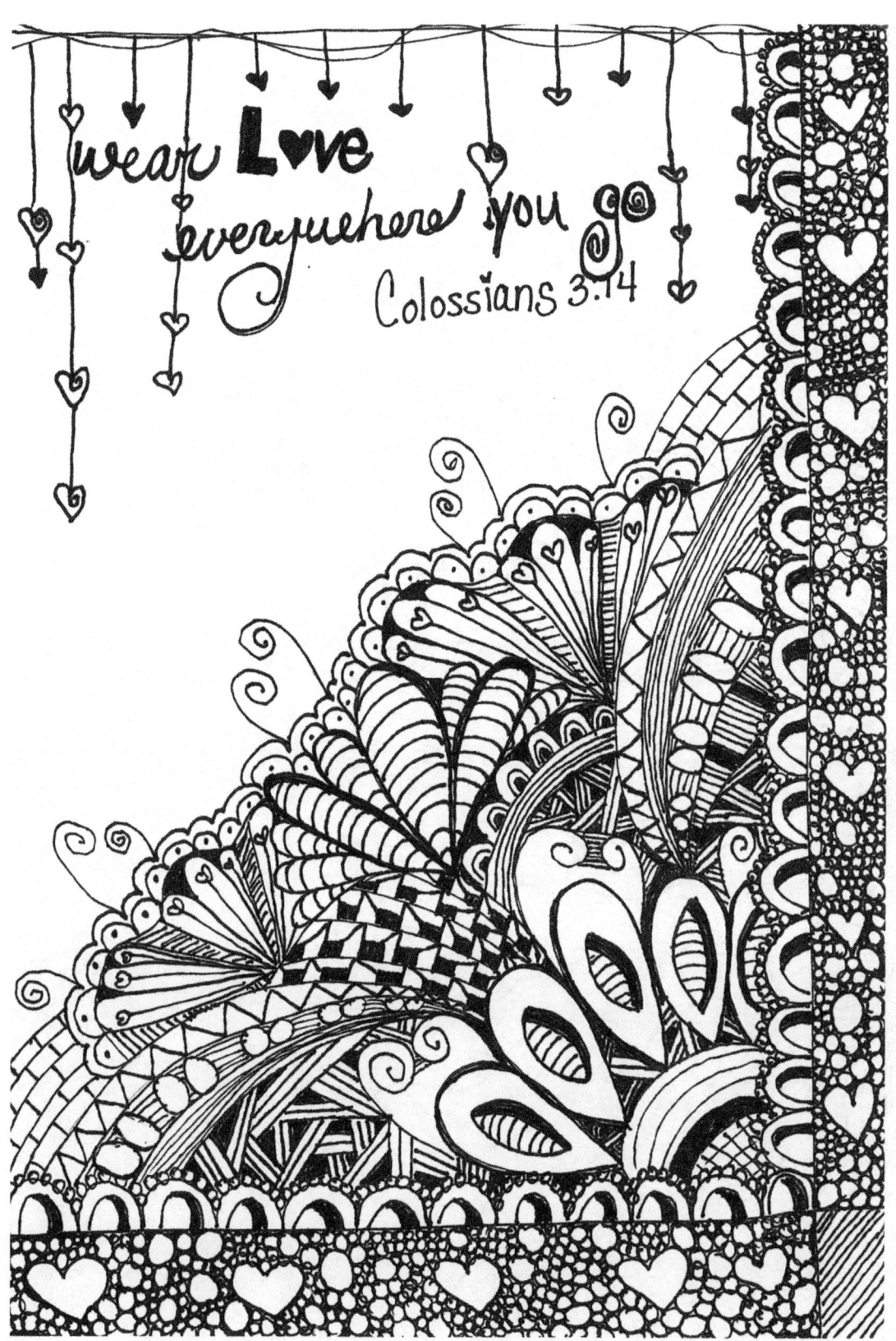

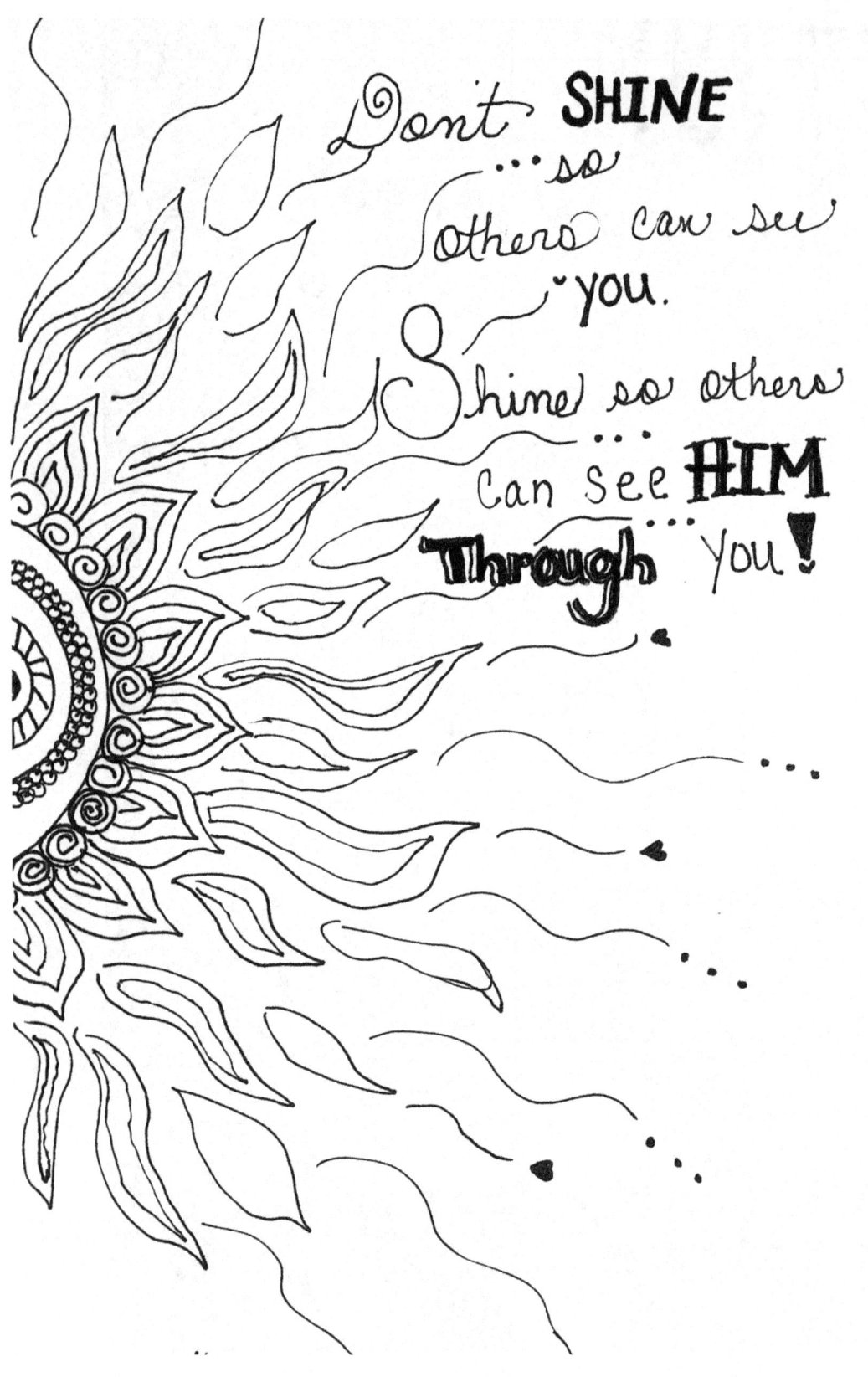

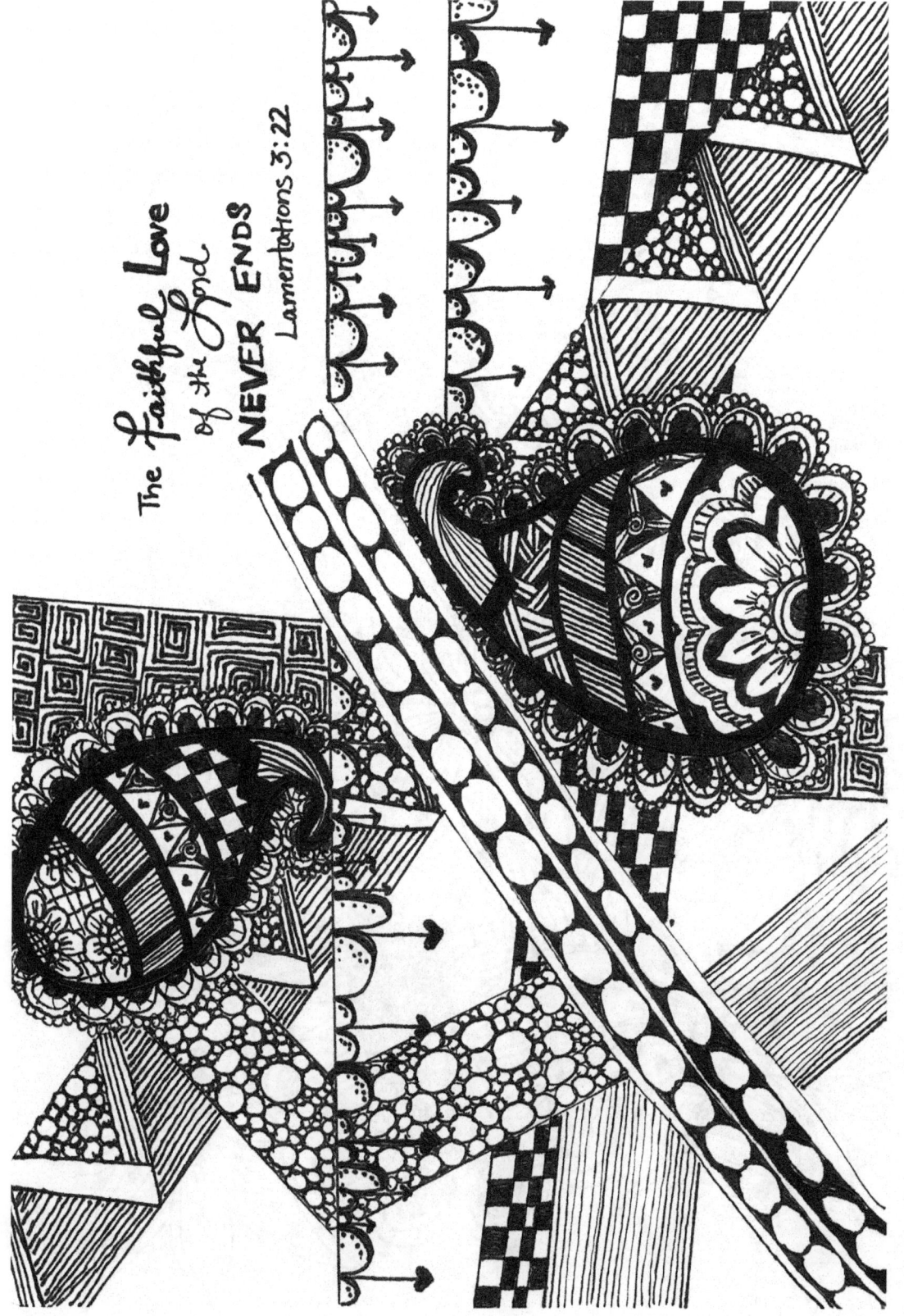

The Faithful Love of the Lord NEVER ENDS
Lamentations 3:22

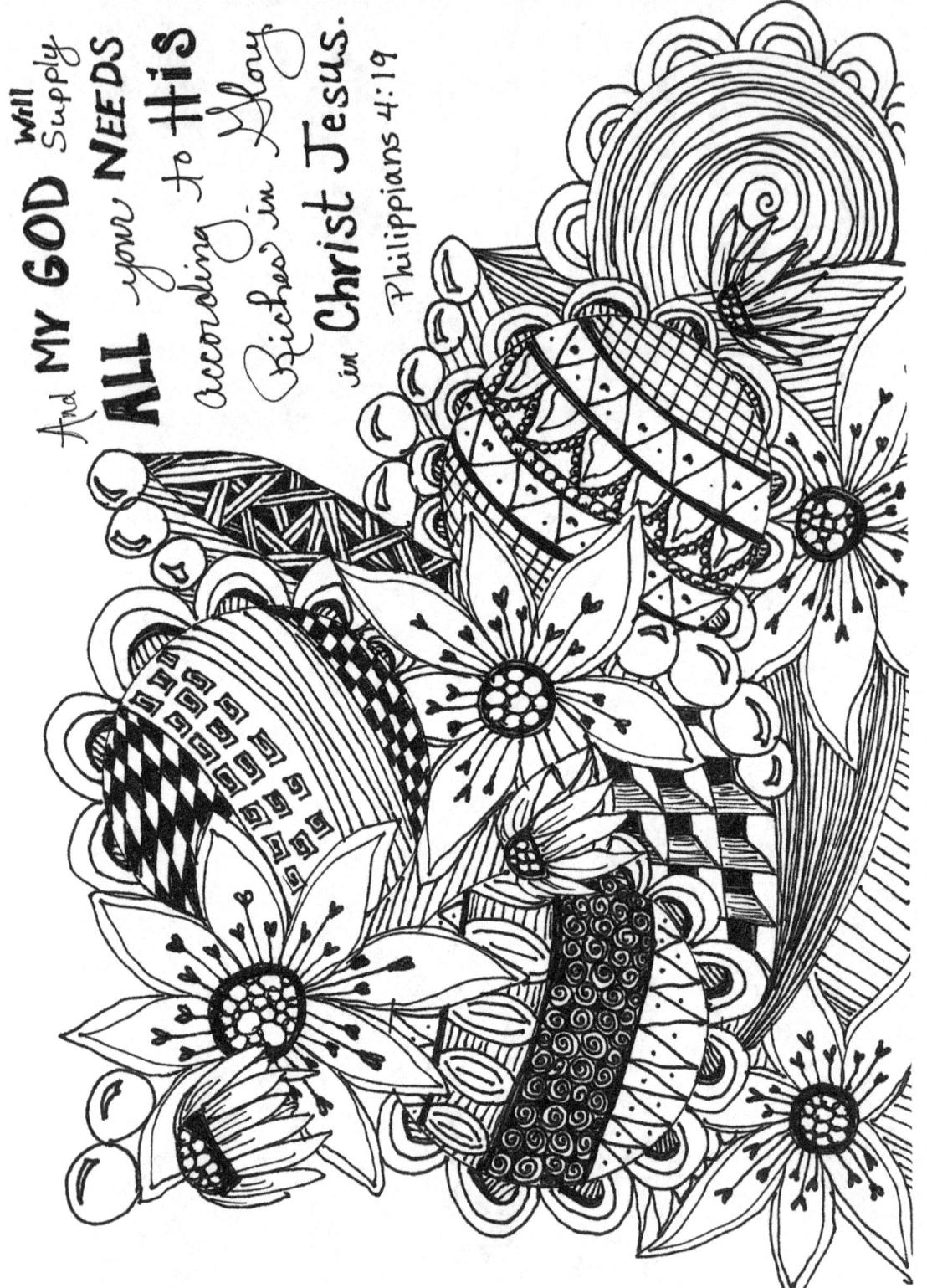

And MY GOD will supply ALL your NEEDS according to His Riches in Glory in Christ Jesus. Philippians 4:19

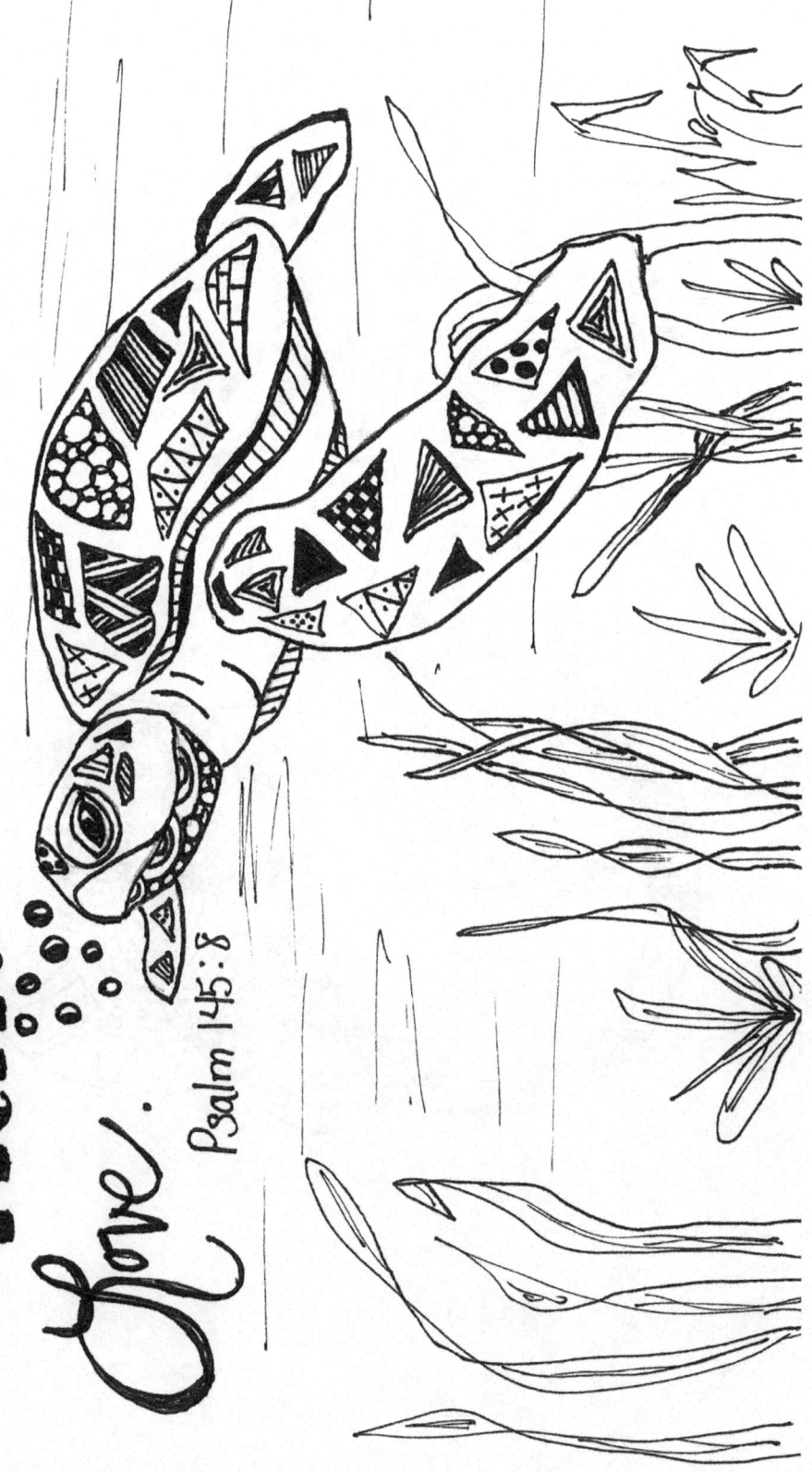

The LORD is gracious and compassionate SLOW to ANGER and rich in love. Psalm 145:8

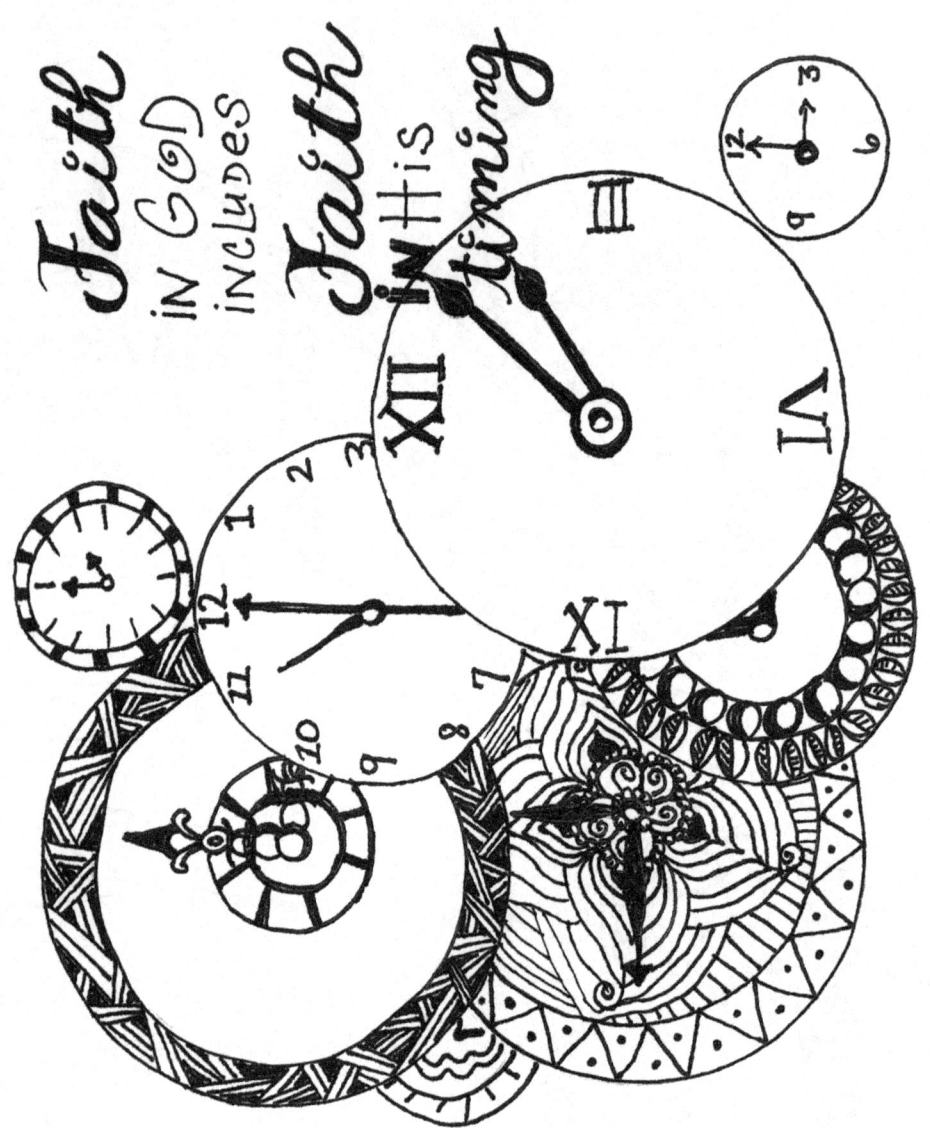

Faith in GOD includes

Faith in His timing

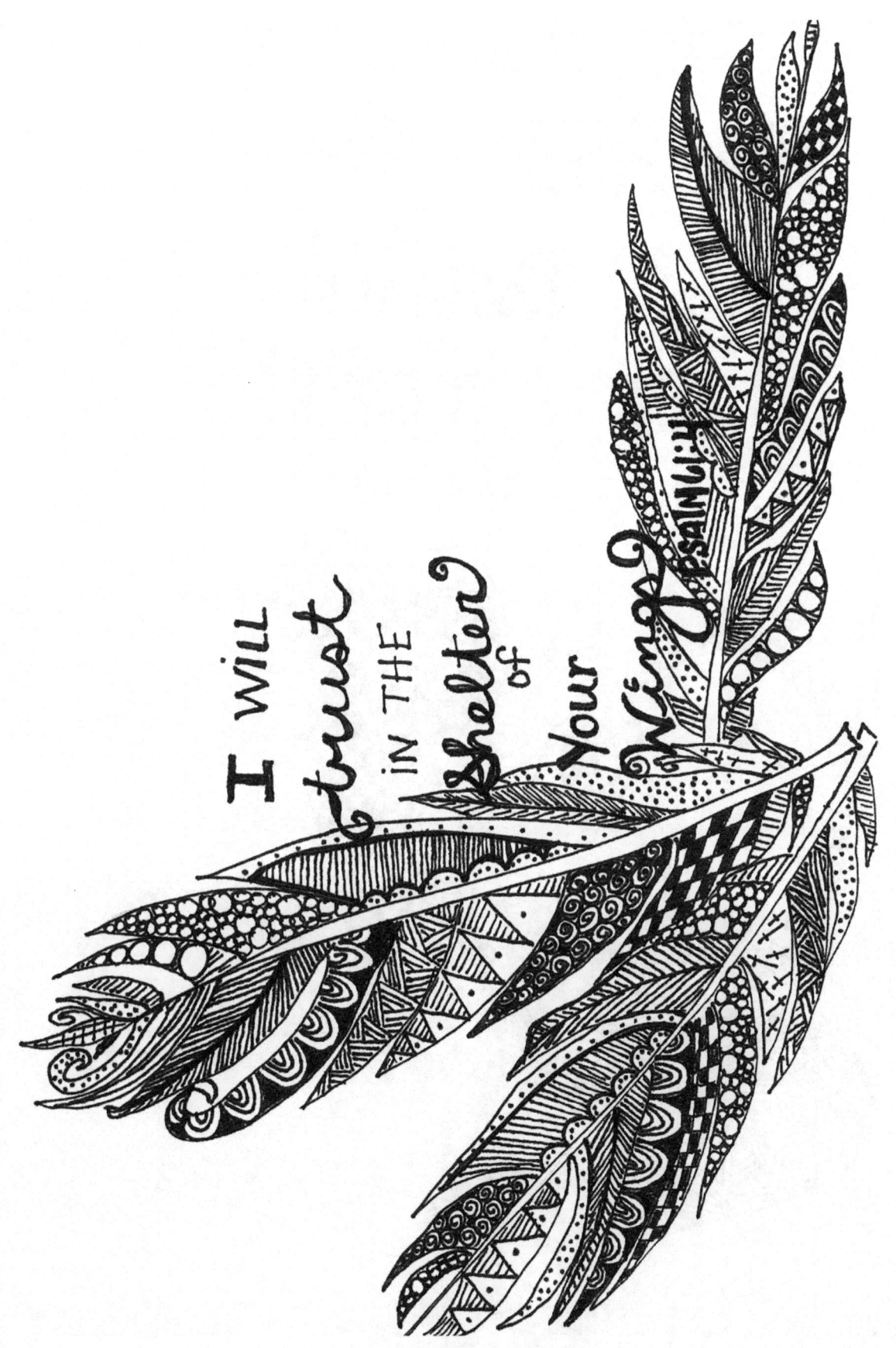

Perfect Love
Casts out
Fear
I John 4:18

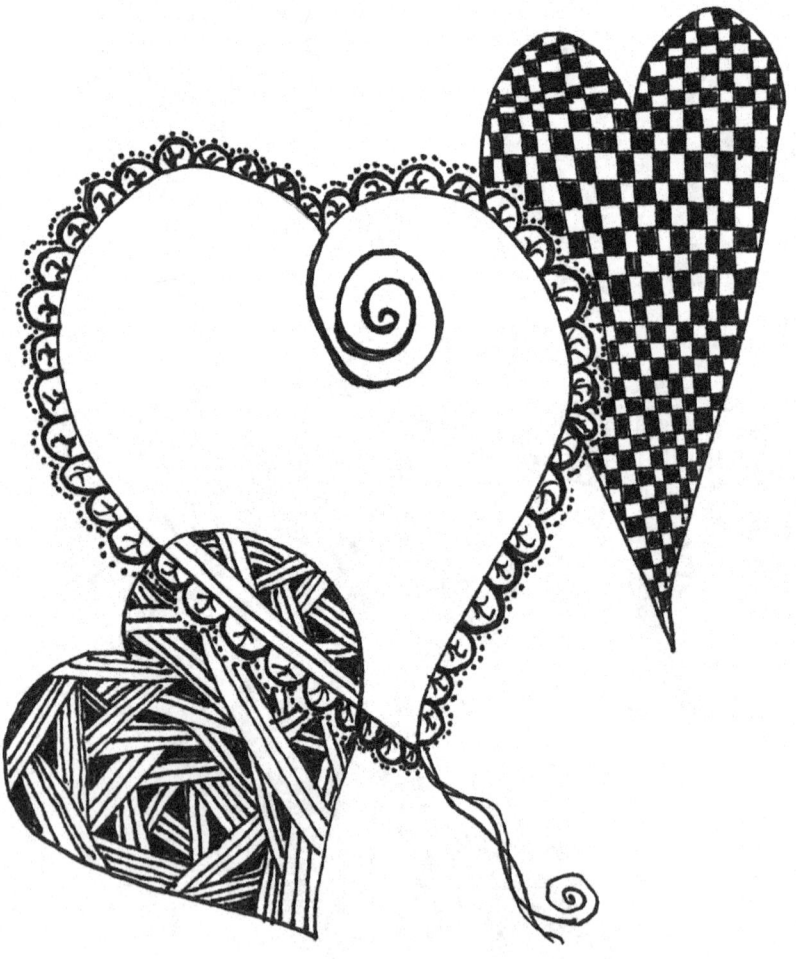

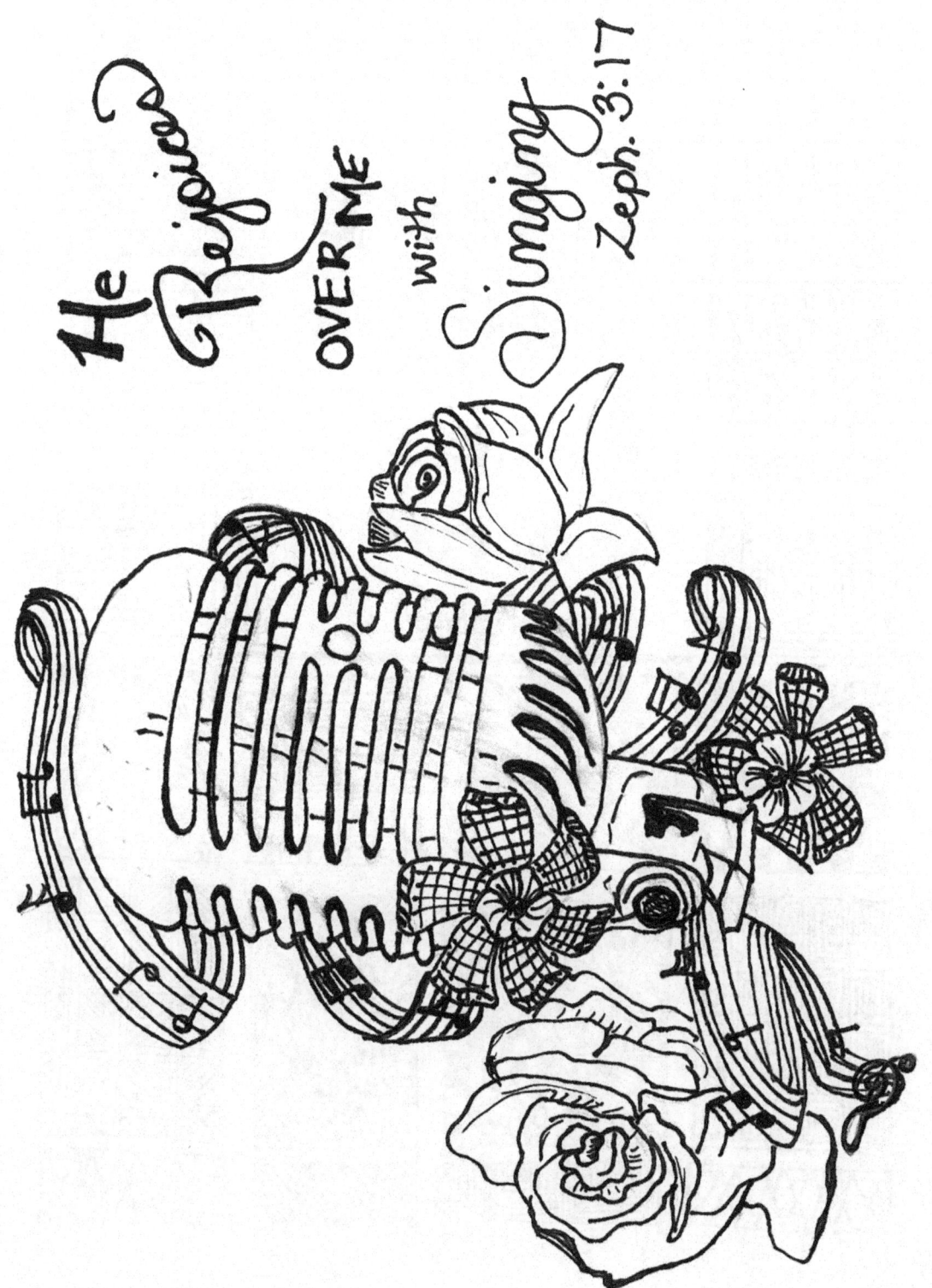

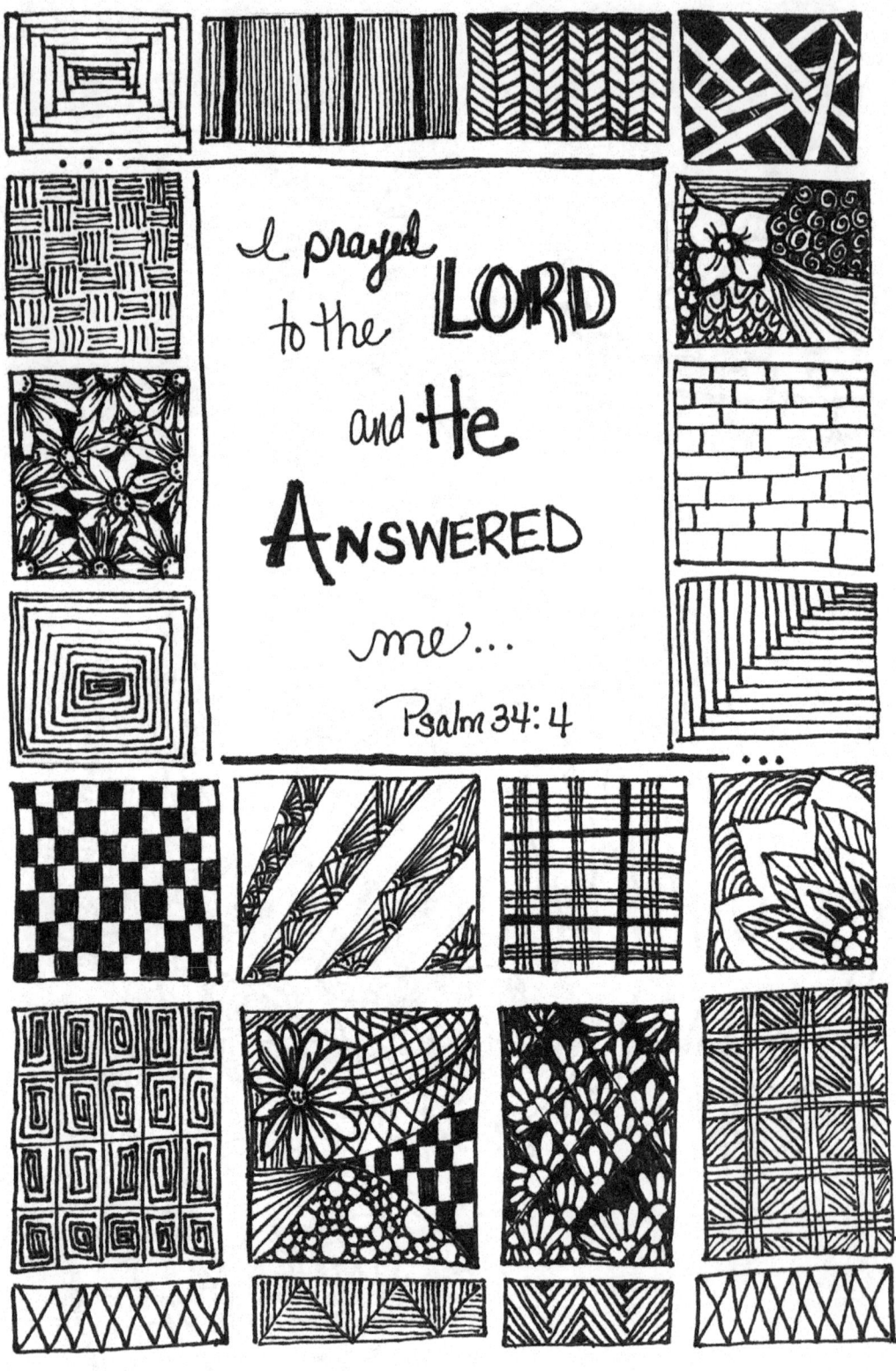

I prayed to the **LORD** and **He ANSWERED** me...

Psalm 34:4

Whooo can seperate US from the Love of God?

Romans 8:38

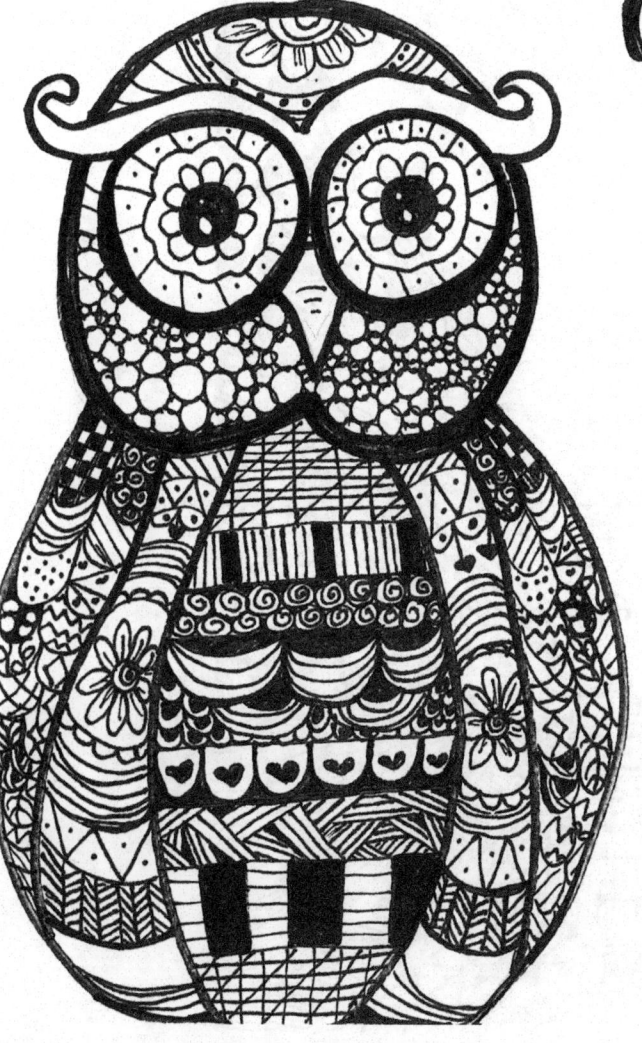

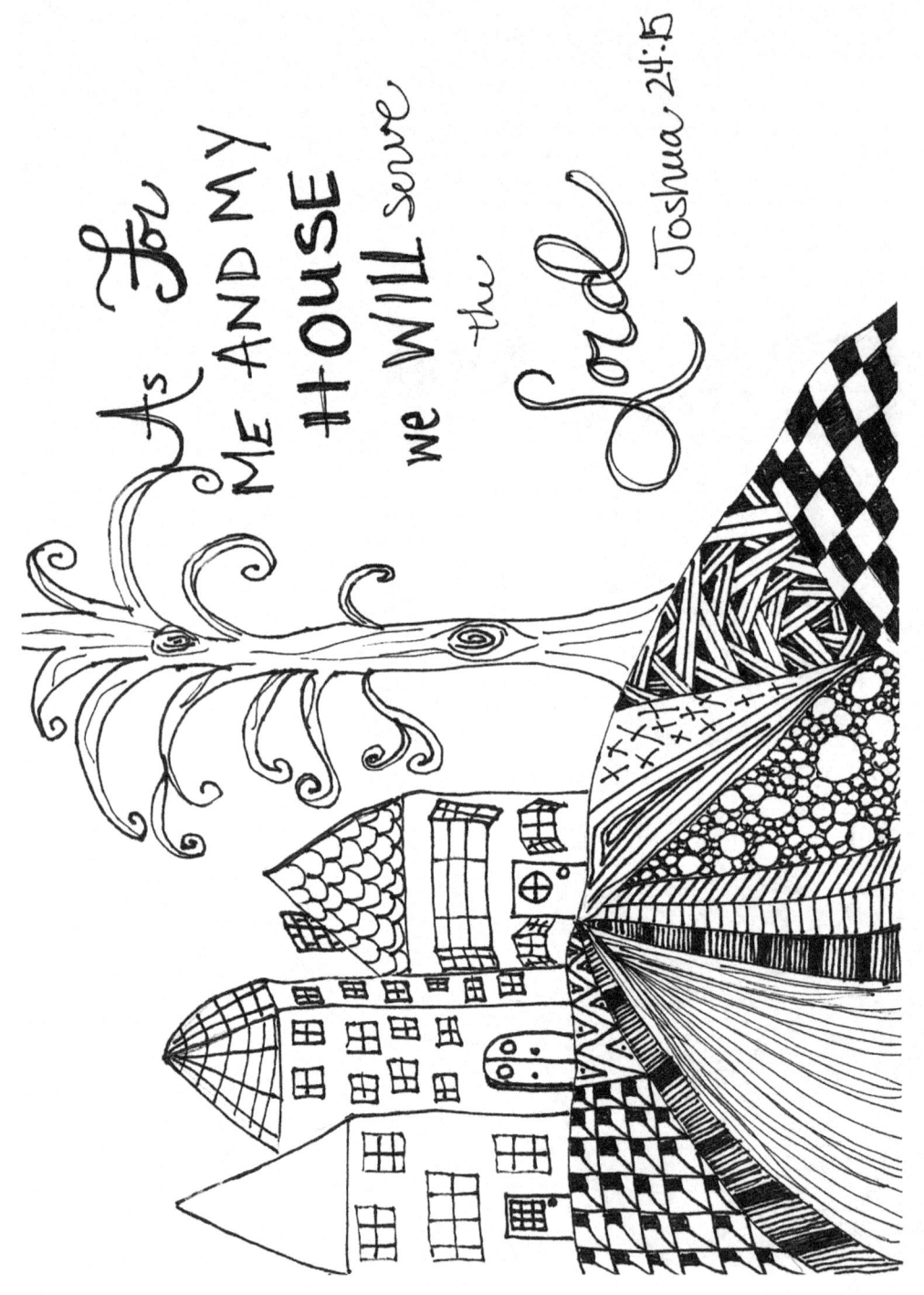

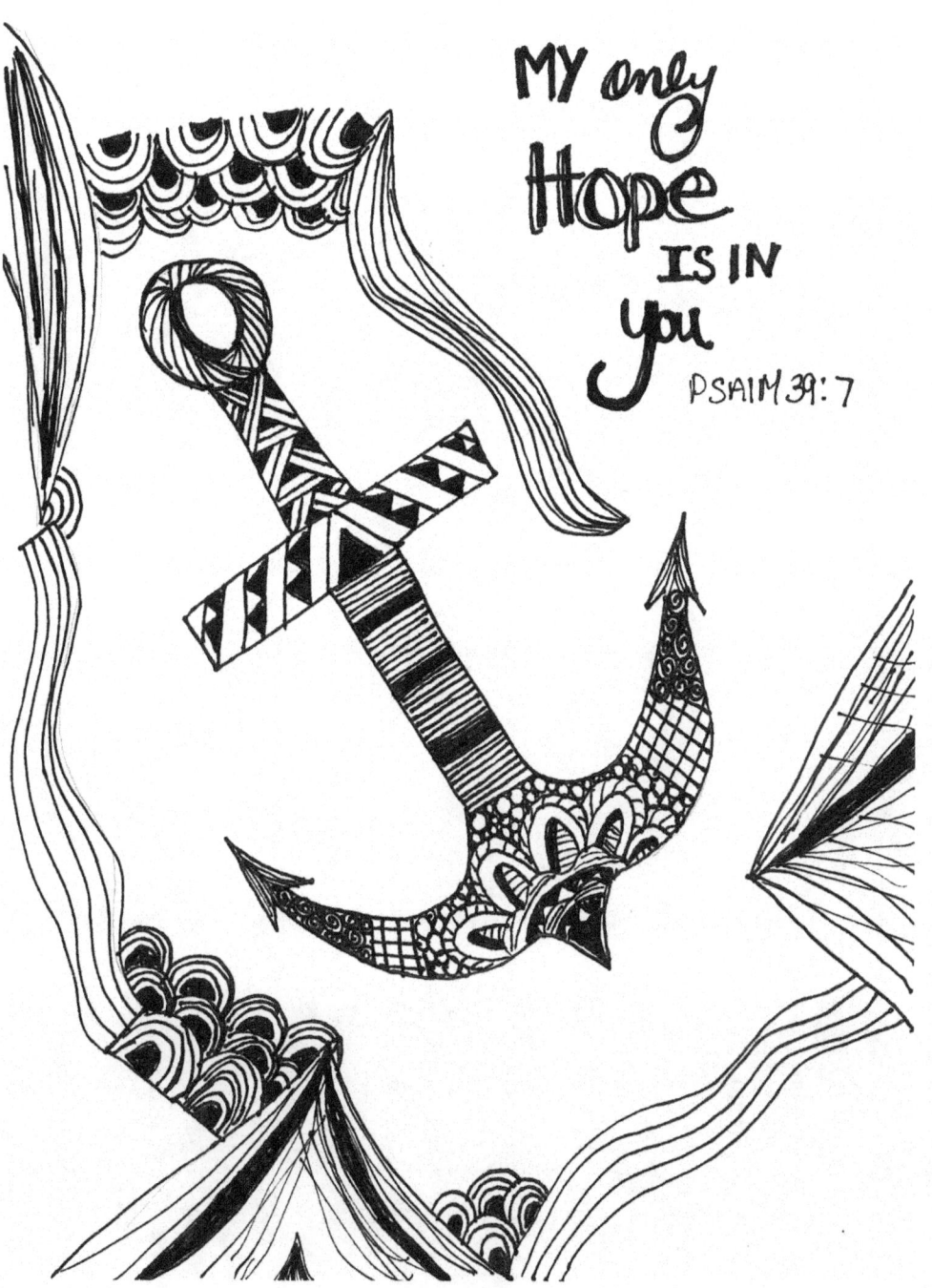

MY only Hope IS IN You PSALM 39:7